Facts About the Anaconda

By Lisa Strattin

© 2016 Lisa Strattin

Revised 2022 © Lisa Strattin

# FREE BOOK

## FREE FOR ALL SUBSCRIBERS

**LisaStrattin.com/Subscribe-Here**

# BOX SET

- **FACTS ABOUT THE POISON DART FROGS**
- **FACTS ABOUT THE THREE TOED SLOTH**
  - **FACTS ABOUT THE RED PANDA**
  - **FACTS ABOUT THE SEAHORSE**
  - **FACTS ABOUT THE PLATYPUS**
  - **FACTS ABOUT THE REINDEER**
  - **FACTS ABOUT THE PANTHER**
- **FACTS ABOUT THE SIBERIAN HUSKY**

# LisaStrattin.com/BookBundle

# Facts for Kids Picture Books by Lisa Strattin

Little Blue Penguin, Vol 92

Chipmunk, Vol 5

Frilled Lizard, Vol 39

Blue and Gold Macaw, Vol 13

Poison Dart Frogs, Vol 50

Blue Tarantula, Vol 115

African Elephants, Vol 8

Amur Leopard, Vol 89

Sabre Tooth Tiger, Vol 167

Baboon, Vol 174

Sign Up for New Release Emails Here

LisaStrattin.com/subscribe-here

**\*\*COVER IMAGE\*\***

https://www.flickr.com/photos/sakeeb/23921890193/

**\*\*ADDITIONAL IMAGES\*\***

https://www.flickr.com/photos/erikkristensen/8615082240/

https://www.flickr.com/photos/edenpictures/51202427380/

https://www.flickr.com/photos/philliecasablanca/2051884835

https://www.flickr.com/photos/philliecasablanca/2051883607

https://www.flickr.com/photos/erikkristensen/8612349013/

https://www.flickr.com/photos/143373510@N02/51895737614/

https://www.flickr.com/photos/ctam/2659904418/

https://www.flickr.com/photos/brindle95/9444543835/

https://www.flickr.com/photos/davelonsdale/6159211403/

https://www.flickr.com/photos/jubeiz/114647189/

# Contents

# WHAT IS THE ANACONDA?

The Anaconda is a large snake found in the tropics of South America. Anaconda implies a group of snakes for most people, but the name refers to the Green Anaconda, the largest snake and second longest in the world.

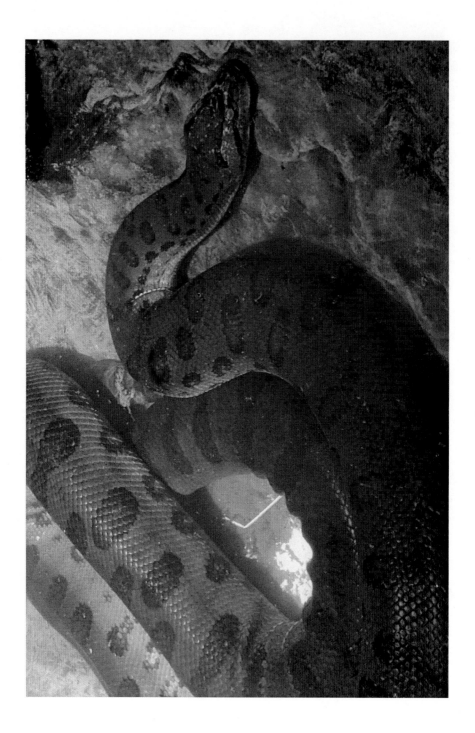

# LIFE CYCLE

The life of the Anaconda begins when a female and a male Anaconda mate. Mating takes place at habitats that are typically swampy areas. Mating takes several hours given the muddy grounds; the Anacondas slither around as they mate. The male fertilizes the eggs and development begins. Shortly after this, the female gives birth to young ones. Anacondas are reptiles and they have 20 to 50 babies at one time. The babies can measure up to 23 inches long and they start surviving on their own immediately after birth. This means they can live without their parent's help!

# HABITAT

Anacondas live in marshes, swamps, and slow-moving streams, mainly in the tropical rainforest of the Orinoco basins and the Amazon. Though they are cumbersome on land, Anacondas are sleek and stealthy in water. Their nasal openings and eyes are perfect for the water environment they live in since these openings are on top of their head. This allows them to submerge in water, hiding, as they wait for their prey.

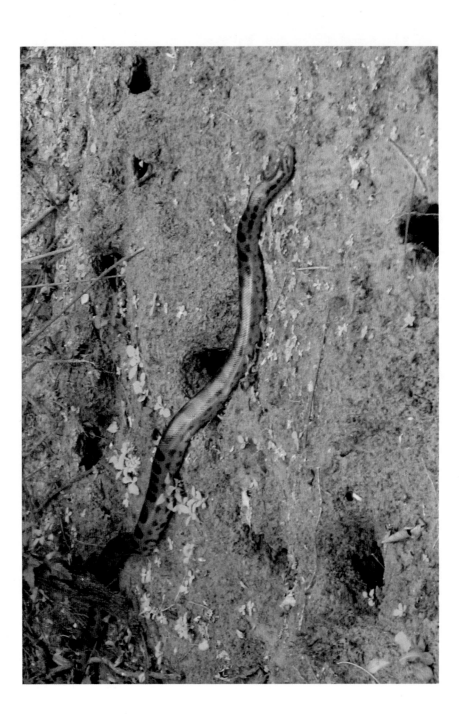

## CHARACTERISTICS

The Green Anaconda is a member of the boa family; it is the largest snake in the world. The cousin to the Green Anaconda is the Reticulated Python that reaches greater lengths, but the Anaconda's girth makes it makes it twice as heavy as these python cousins.

# CATCHING THEIR FOOD

They are nonvenomous constrictors; they coil their muscular bodies around a meal and squeeze until their prey dies.

Stretchy ligaments allow the jaws of an Anaconda to open their mouth very wide, so they can eat large animals and swallow them whole. To help in swallowing, most adult anacondas have more than 100 teeth that are curved.

# SIZE

Females are generally larger than the males. Other species of snakes found in South America; are smaller compared to the Green Anaconda, Dark-Spotted, Yellow, and Bolivian varieties.

Green Anacondas usually weigh more than 550 pounds, they grow to more than 29 feet long, and their diameter (the length around their body) is more than 12 inches!

# DIET

The enormous size of Anacondas is due to their diet of wild pigs, birds, deer, caimans, capybara, turtles and even jaguars.

# BABIES HUNT THEIR OWN FOOD

The babies hunt for their meals; they feed on small prey until they grow to a larger size and are experienced enough to kill bigger prey. The average life span of an anaconda is between 10 to 30 years. As they grow, they develop organs that help to sense heat from their surroundings.

# SUITABILITY AS A PET

A captive bred Anaconda has the potential to be a calm pet if properly raised. However, they do grow large, and you must not underestimate their strength. Anacondas are not recommended for people new to snake handling. Anyone deciding to keep one as a pet must have prior experience of handling large constrictors.

A good choice for an experienced reptile owner is a captive-bred Green Anaconda. Also, young Anacondas have a lower probability of carrying foreign bacteria and parasites to their new home. Another merit of keeping a very young one for a pet is that the snake can easily get adjusted to the new environment. Snake keepers benefit from keeping a young Anaconda since they will get more knowledge on the raising, history, quirks, disposition, and normal behaviors.

A point to note is that keeping an Anaconda is an enormous commitment. A Green Anaconda will need a large room and particular care and attention. Any anaconda will still get quite large, and this calls for more care than other, smaller snakes.

If you are not very experienced with snakes as pets, a Boa Constrictor or Burmese Python will make a better first-choice for you. These other two varieties are still impressive in size but require less special knowledge when you start keeping snakes as pets.

# COLOR ME

# COLOR ME

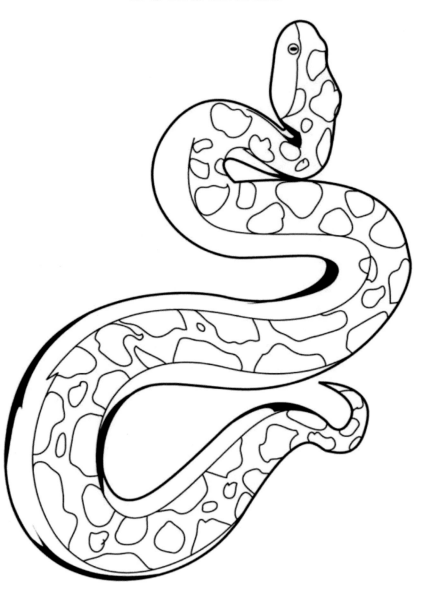

# COLOR ME

# COLOR ME

# COLOR ME

# COLOR ME

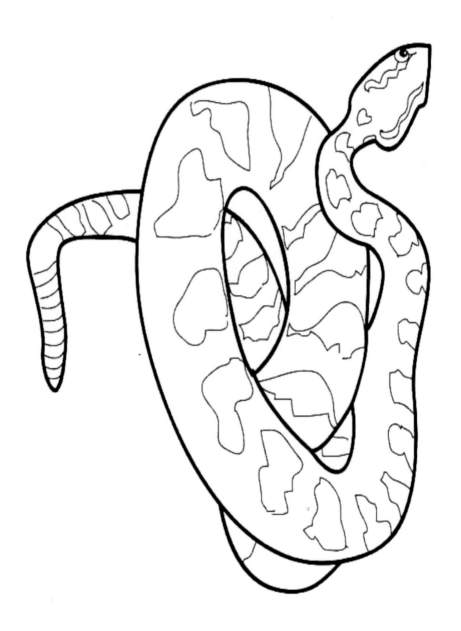

# COLOR ME

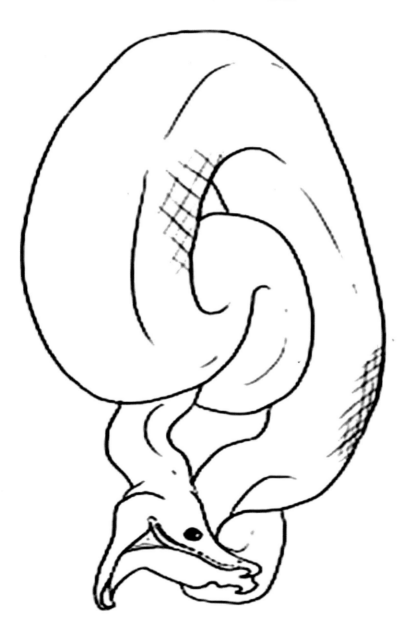

# COLOR ME

# COLOR ME

# COLOR ME

Please leave me a review here:

*LisaStrattin.com/Review-Vol-11*

**For more Kindle Downloads Visit Lisa Strattin Author Page on Amazon Author Central**

*amazon.com/author/lisastrattin*

**To see upcoming titles, visit my website at LisaStrattin.com– most books available on Kindle!**

*LisaStrattin.com*

# FREE BOOK

## FOR ALL SUBSCRIBERS – SIGN UP NOW

**LisaStrattin.com/Subscribe-Here**

**LisaStrattin.com/Facebook**

**LisaStrattin.com/Youtube**